Water, Land and Air

Pat Malone

This is what the Earth looks like from space.

2

Can you see how blue it is?
The blue part is water.

The  is mostly water.

People need water to live.

Can you see the brown and green parts of the Earth?
The brown and green parts are land.

Only part of the Earth is land.

People live on the land.

9

Air is all around the Earth.

You can't see it, but it's there.

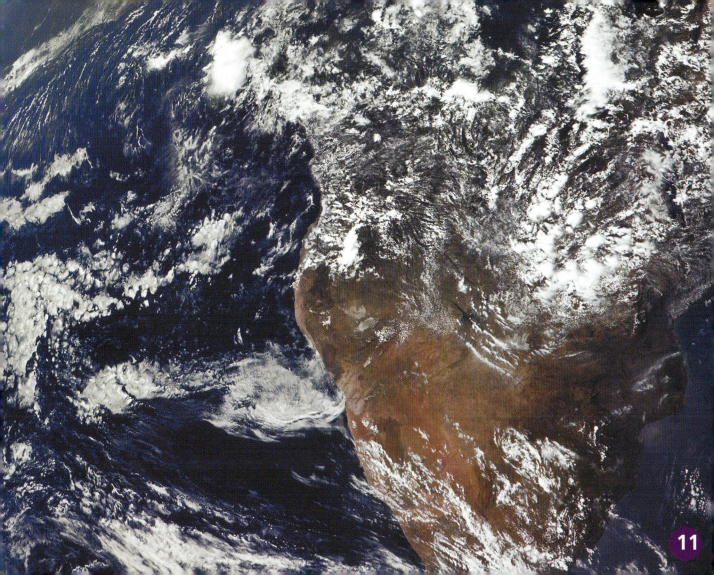

People breathe the air.

Water, land and air
are all things people need.